A UNITED METHODIST IS . . .

Abingdon Press
Nashville

A UNITED METHODIST IS . . .

Writer: Pam Buchholz
Editor: Marcia J. Stoner
Production Editor: Janet Patterson
Designer: Randall Butler
Cover Design: Tony Kougios

ISBN 978-0-687-64761-3
PACP00384947-01

09 10 11 12 13 14 15 16 17 18 — 10 9 8 7 6 5 4 3 2 1
Manufactured in the United States of America

CONTENTS

ABOUT THE WRITER

Reverend Pamela Buchholz is an ordained deacon and has served in the area of Christian Education for 25 years. She earned an M.A. in Christian Education from Garrett-Evangelical Theological Seminary and serves at First United Methodist Church in Midland, Michigan. She loves God and all of God's children.

Pam has written for Exploring Faith, Live It!, and Live B.I.G. She is also the author of *Choosing to Be a Christian* and *What Is a Christian?*

HOW TO USE THIS BOOK

A United Methodist Is . . . is a short-term study consisting of six sessions that each can be adapted from 45 minutes to an hour and a half. It introduces tweens to a brief history of The United Methodist Church. It helps tweens begin to understand what being a United Methodist means.

A United Methodist Is . . . can be used as a pre-confirmation curriculum that encourages tweens to take the next step in beginning the process of committing to full membership in the Christian denomination that is The United Methodist Church.

A United Methodist Is . . . can be used with tweens in a variety of settings. It is designed to be used with fifth- and sixth-grade students, with optional use up to seventh grade.

SETTINGS

- Sunday school
- Wednesday nights
- Short-term studies coinciding with other short-term church events
- Study for those new to The Untied Methodist Church
- Pre-confirmation

USE WITH
WHAT IS A UNITED METHODIST?

The participant's piece is *What Is a United Methodist?* This book of puzzles, questions, and challenges is meant for use with *A United Methodist Is . . .* during the sessions. It can also be used as a stand-alone piece and makes a wonderful gift, especially for those entering a confirmation program.

THE STORY BEGINS

THE MAIN IDEA

John Wesley is the father of Methodism, and he believed in personal holiness and social action.

THE GOALS

Tweens will:
• Learn about John Wesley's childhood and the Holy Club.
• Practice self-examination as was done in the Holy Club.
• Discover some of the ways Methodists served those in need.

THE BIBLE

Psalm 119:105, Matthew 25:31-40, Romans 7:15, Hebrews 3:12-14 (CEV)

THE PLAN

Get Ready

Today it is common to find a church by shopping for the one with the best music, the most exciting preaching, and the most active youth group. It is becoming less common for people to have a strong denominational tie. *A United Methodist Is . . .* will help tweens understand and appreciate what it means to be a United Methodist. The matching game in this session is the primary way they will hear and learn about John Wesley's family background. Help tweens make correlations between the events of early Methodism

PREPARE YOUR SESSION

STUFF TO COLLECT:

☐ **Bibles**
☐ markers
☐ nametags (or pins and paper to make nametags)
☐ scissors
☐ pencils
☐ two chairs
☐ activities list (sidebar, p. 10)
☐ **Reproducible 1A, p. 11**
☐ **Reproducible 1B, p. 12**
☐ **Reproducible 1C, p. 54**
☐ **What Is a United Methodist?**

For cool ❄ *options:*

☐ thumbtacks
☐ Velcro
☐ bulletin board or felt board
☐ pencils
☐ **What Is a United Methodist?**

STUFF TO DO:

1. Make photocopies of Reproducible 1A and cut cards apart (four sets).
2. Make photocopies of Reproducibles 1B and 1C.

An optional activity next week is to have one or more people come in to share their faith stories. Think of people from your congregation who would be willing to share their witness, and invite them to join you for all or part of the session.

STUFF—NICKNAMES:

- [ ] markers

- [ ] nametags (or pins and paper to make nametags)

and events they know of from their study of history. John Wesley's life spans most of the eighteenth century, from 1703 to 1791. During this same span was the American Revolution, the development of the slave trade, and the beginnings of the Industrial Revolution. It was a time of great political and economic change during which the Methodists played an important role in the area of social justice and reform.

John Wesley felt called to nurture his own soul continually and to care for the bodies and souls of the lost and the marginalized. His strict rules of behavior are a challenge to Christians today. Even his first rule for the Holy Club, to rise early, could be a challenge for many tweens. Wesley knew the importance of a small group in helping Christians grow and be held accountable. Talk with your tweens about ways they can find that kind of support in your church family. This might be through a Sunday school class, youth group, or just a group of two or three who commit to pray for one another and check in with one another. You can play an important role in the tweens' lives also. Be ready to listen to their needs and support them on their faith journeys.

GET STARTED

Nicknames Time: 5-7 minutes

Welcome tweens and give tweens and adult leaders nametags. Tell them to put their full given name at the top and underneath it the name they prefer to be called.

Go around for introductions, with each person saying what is on his or her nametag and one thing that is positive about your church.

Ask: How many people go by their full given first name?

Say: It is very common to go by some kind of nickname. We may have other nicknames that only our family or close friends call us.

Say: United Methodism begins with the story of John Wesley. John Wesley is remembered as the father of Methodism, but he never meant to start a new church. He just wanted to see the people in his own church live out the Gospel as fully as

ossible. During college, John Wesley and his friends were given the nickname "Methodists."

Ask: Why do you think a group would be called Methodist?

Say: It was because they followed a strict method in living the Christian life. We will learn more about that over the next few weeks.

Beginnings: Concentration Time: 10–15 minutes

Copy and cut apart the "Methodist Beginnings Matching Cards" (**Reproducible 1A—p. 11**). (Four sets)

Count off by fours to divide into four groups. Give each group a set of cards. Someone from each group mixes up the cards and spreads them out face-down. Players then take turns turning over a pair of cards (one of each kind). Each time a card is turned, the player must read aloud what it says. *This step is a key part of the learning process.* Look for the words in all capital letters on each card to tell if you have a match. Keep the pair and take another turn if it is a match. Whether or not the next pair is a match, the play then moves to the next player.

DIG IN

Methodism Begins Time: 15 minutes

Review the early history of John Wesley by reading through the "Methodist Beginnings Matching Cards" (**Reproducible 1A—p. 11**). Read each name or phrase and see if tweens can identify it. Fill in the definitions as needed.

Say: Susanna Wesley gave birth to nineteen children, but only ten survived infancy. Life was hard for the Wesleys. John's father, Samuel, was so poor that he had trouble providing for his large family. He was not a great money manager and was even sent to debtors' prison for a time for not paying his debts. Samuel was a pastor in the Church of England. But it was John's mother, Susanna, who served as John's lifelong spiritual advisor. While Samuel was unpopular with the people of Epworth, Susanna was well-loved for her ministry to the poor and her leadership in the "religious society" meetings that she held in her home.

TIP: The concentration game does not assume or require any prior knowledge. The game is a learning process that will introduce tweens to some of the early history of Methodism.

STUFF—BEGINNINGS: CONCENTRATION

- ❑ **Reproducible 1A**
- ❑ scissors

COOL OPTION: Enlarge the cards and use thumbtacks or Velcro to put them on a large bulletin board or felt board. Get dramatic and play the game-show host, with members of each team taking turns choosing a pair of cards.

STUFF—METHODISM BEGINS:

- ❑ **Reproducible 1A**
- ❑ **What Is a United Methodist?**
- ❑ pencils

Say: John and his siblings grew up in a home in which prayer and Bible reading were an important part of every day. Both John and his younger brother, Charles, went to Oxford University, where they studied to become ministers in the Church of England, like their father. While at Oxford, Charles started a small group that met together weekly for prayer and Bible study. John soon became the leader of the group. John expected the participants to rise early each day, to read the Bible, to pray, and to help those in need.

Ask: Do you think most college students would want to join a group like that? Students in the 1700's were not that different from students today. Only a few joined John's group, while many others made fun of them.

Have tweens complete the word puzzle "Name-calling" (**What Is a United Methodist?—p. 7**) to learn what the other students called John, Charles, and their faithful group members.

Say: Probably most of the students doing the name-calling considered themselves Christians.

Ask: How do you think their practice of Christianity differed from the practice of the members of the Holy Club? What do you think John Wesley would think of Christians today? If a Holy Club were started at your school, would you join?

Bible Basics Time: 15 minutes

Read Psalm 119:105.

Ask: What does that verse mean to you?

Say: John Wesley believed firmly that if the Bible is to be our guide, we must read it regularly and prayerfully, discuss it with other Christians, and live it out in our daily lives.

Ask: How important do you think it is for Christians to read the Bible? Do you read the Bible daily? What do you think is a big challenge to Christians in reading the Bible?

Say: According to a recent study, Americans are becoming biblically illiterate. They may talk a lot about faith and values but fewer and fewer people are actually reading the Bible and taking it seriously.

STUFF—BIBLE BASICS:

❏ **Bibles**

❏ **Reproducible 1B**

❏ pencils

Hand out copies of "Rate Your Bible Literacy" (**Reproducible 1B—p. 12**). Give everyone a few minutes to complete the quiz. Then go over the correct answers.

Do an informal survey by having everyone hold up one to ten fingers, with ten being the best and one being the worst, to rate their own Bible literacy.

Say: John Wesley and his band of Methodists knew the importance of Bible reading, prayer, and group support in helping Christians grow in faith. John took the Bible seriously, and so his reading of the Gospels led him into action.

Read Matthew 25:31-40.

Ask: If you are going to take the Bible seriously, what does this Scripture lesson tell you to do?

Say: Life in England in the 1700's was changing quickly. The population boomed, making for crowded conditions and shortages of food and supplies. It was the beginning of the Industrial Revolution. There was a big movement of people going from the country to the city in search of work. What they found was often worse than what they'd left.

Say: John Wesley tried to live out the teaching of Matthew 25:35-36 by providing food, clothing, and medical care to those in need. He organized Methodist Societies that raised money to provide for the poor. They visited the sick and those in prison. The Methodists took the love of Christ to places where most people would not willingly go.

God and Me   Time: 15 minutes

Say: One of the things the Methodists did in the Holy Club and later in the Methodist Societies was hold one another accountable. One way they did this was to go through a checklist together of how they were doing in living in the way of Christ. This accountability was not done to make people feel bad, but to help them see areas of their lives where they still needed to grow. The good news was that these life changes were not something they had to work out on their own. They had the support of one another, but most of all, they had God's help.

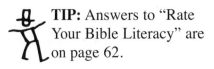**TIP:** Answers to "Rate Your Bible Literacy" are on page 62.

✳ **COOL OPTION:** Learn more about life in Wesley's England by completing "Not So Jolly Old England" (**What Is a United Methodist?—pp. 8-9**).

STUFF—GOD AND ME:

❏ **Reproducible 1C**

✳ **COOL OPTION:** Have tweens complete "The Least of These" word search **(What Is a United Methodist? —p. 10)** to learn some of the groups of people to whom the Methodists ministered.

"Taking it Further" Activities List:
1. going to church
2. playing soccer
3. playing a musical instrument
4. singing in the church choir
5. going to Sunday school
6. attending an all-night party with friends
7. seeing an R-rated movie
8. playing video games
9. going to church youth group
10. praying
11. surfing the Net
12. posting on Facebook
13. reading the Bible
14. lots of one-on-one time with someone of the opposite sex
15. talking to a trusted Christian adult

STUFF—WORSHIP:

❏ **Bible**

STUFF—TAKING IT FURTHER:

❏ two chairs

❏ activities list above

Hand out "Asking the Tough Questions" **(Reproducible 1C—p. 54).**

Say: Imagine we are one of Wesley's Holy Clubs. Listen as I read each question aloud and take a moment in silence to think about how you would answer.

Read through the questions. Then form groups of three or four people. Invite tweens each to choose at least one question to answer honestly with the group.

Ask: Was that hard to do?

Say: It can be hard to see clearly both our strengths and weaknesses. The time of accountability was also a time to celebrate ways the group members were growing in faith. No one is perfect.

WORSHIP
Time: 2 minutes

Ask a volunteer to read Romans 7:15.

Say: Paul wrote those words to express the frustration of failing to live as he knew Christ desired. Paul gives thanks for the forgiveness we have in Jesus and the strength we have through the Holy Spirit to become more faithful Christians.

Close with prayer, including a general confession of sin and asking for God's help in living a more faithful life.

TAKING IT FURTHER
Time: 15 minutes

Have everyone line up across the middle of the room. Put a chair at either end to mark this as the center. Explain that you will read through a list of activities. If it is something they think would make their lives holier, they should take a step forward. If it has the potential to pull them away from God, they should take a step backward. If they think it would have no effect, they can stay where they are. (See list in sidebar to upper left.)

Say: Living a Christian life is all about balance. To develop our gifts and be challenged to be thinking Christians, we need to participate in a variety of activities with a variety of people.

Reproducible 1A

METHODIST BEGINNINGS MATCHING CARDS

JOHN WESLEY	**JOHN WESLEY** was born in England in 1703 and is remembered as the father of Methodism. However, until his death in 1791, John remained a minister in the Church of England.	When John Wesley was a boy, the parsonage at Epworth caught on **FIRE**, trapping him in an upstairs bedroom.
EPWORTH		
SAMUEL	**EPWORTH** is the little town in England where John Wesley lived as a boy. John grew up in the Epworth parsonage because his father was the village "parson" or preacher.	After neighbors formed a human ladder to rescue John from the fire at Epworth, his mother called John **"A BRAND SNATCHED FROM THE BURNING,"** and she dedicated his life to God.
SUSANNA		
FIFTH BIRTHDAY	John's father, **SAMUEL**, was a priest in the Church of England. He was not popular in the village because he was very strict.	John's younger brother, **CHARLES**, was John's partner in ministry and the writer of over 5,000 hymns.
FIRE		
"A BRAND SNATCHED FROM THE BURNING"	John's mother, **SUSANNA**, was his first teacher and continued to guide him in his ministry throughout her life.	While a student at Oxford University near London, John and brother Charles started the **HOLY CLUB**. Members of the group met regularly for devotions, prayer, and to hold one another accountable for living the Christian faith.
CHARLES		
HOLY CLUB	In the Wesley home, a child's **FIFTH BIRTHDAY** was very special. That was the day each child learned to read with mother, Susanna, as the teacher.	Like his father, John Wesley was a minister in the **CHURCH OF ENGLAND**, which was established in 1534 by King Henry VIII. Henry VIII led the break from the Catholic Church when the Pope would not approve the annulment of his marriage.
CHURCH OF ENGLAND		

Reproducible 1B
RATE YOUR BIBLE LITERACY

1. Name the four Gospels:

2. What book of the Bible tells a story of the creation of the world?

3. What are the first nine words of the 23rd Psalm?

4. Who heard God speaking in a burning bush?

5. Who baptized Jesus in the River Jordan?

6. Jesus told his disciples, "If any want to become my followers, let them deny themselves and take up their _____ and follow me."

Match these people with the event:

▲ Noah   Met Jesus when he was blinded on the Damascus Road

▲ Jacob   Denied Jesus three times

▲ Joseph   Betrayed Jesus for thirty pieces of silver

▲ Isaiah   Was shown the rainbow as a sign of God's covenant

▲ Judas   Name was changed to Israel; was father of twelve sons

▲ Moses   Sold by his brothers into slavery in Egypt

▲ Paul   Told Pharaoh, "Let my people go."

▲ Peter   A prophet who told of a Messiah who would suffer for the people

Number Correct	How You Rate
12–14	Awesome!—You know your Bible stories.
10–11	Average—You have paid attention in Sunday school . . . most of the time.
8–9	Shaky—You know some of God's teachings but could use more study.
less than 8	Weak—It's time to get spiritually fit.

     A UNITED METHODIST IS . . .

A HEART STRANGELY WARMED

THE MAIN IDEA

By God's grace we are saved through faith.

THE GOALS

Tweens will
- hear the story of John Wesley's faith journey.
- recognize that God is with us always, even when we don't feel God's presence.
- understand that while we are called to respond to God's love through actions, we are saved through faith by God's grace.
- learn the General Rules of Methodist Societies.

THE BIBLE

Joshua 1:9, Ephesians 2:8, Romans 1:16

THE PLAN

Get Ready

John Wesley had many dramatic moments in his life, but a spiritual turning point was when he "felt his heart strangely warmed" at a meeting on Aldersgate Street. There may be a United Methodist Church near you named "Aldersgate" in recognition of that moment in Wesley's life. Some consider this John Wesley's "born again" moment, and in many ways it was. The assurance he experienced of salvation as a gift

PREPARE YOUR SESSION
STUFF TO COLLECT:

- ☐ **Bibles**
- ☐ scissors
- ☐ pencils
- ☐ paper
- ☐ guests (See "Look Ahead" on p. 6 and "Faith Stories" on p. 18.)
- ☐ **Reproducible 2A, p. 19**
- ☐ **Reproducible 2B, p. 20**
- ☐ **What Is a United Methodist?**

For cool ❄ *options:*

- ☐ **Bible**
- ☐ markerboard
- ☐ marker
- ☐ index cards
- ☐ pencils
- ☐ paper
- ☐ poster-making supplies

STUFF TO DO:

1. Make a photocopy of Reproducible 2A and cut the cards apart.
2. Make photocopies of Reproducible 2B.

from God, and not something that must be earned, refreshed and renewed his spirit. However, there were many moments before this time, from his upbringing in Epworth to his college days at Oxford, that led him to know Christ as his savior. You may have some in your group who have experienced a dramatic encounter with Christ that has changed their life. You may have others for whom their relationship with Christ has been a gradual journey. Be sure tweens understand that however they come to know Christ, being a Christian is a continuing process that can include steps backward as well as forward.

After John Wesley's Aldersgate experience he heard God calling him to take the gospel to the people, rather than waiting for the people to come to the church. That remains a challenge for the church today. Talk with tweens about places where the church might take the gospel in your community. Remind them that Wesley not only preached the Word, he took food and medicine to people, taught them to read, and even helped them start businesses. Wesley shared the good news through words and actions so people could catch the spirit of Christ's love.

You may want to invite in some guests to share their own faith stories with the class. Whether or not you do this, always look for opportunities to share out of your own experience with Christ. The encounters John Wesley had with Jesus may feel like ancient history to tweens. Let them know that Jesus continues to work in the lives of believers in big ways and small.

GET STARTED

Holy Charades   Time: 10 minutes

Copy and cut apart the "Holy Charades Cards" (Reproducible 2A—p. 19).

You may play the game as one group or as two teams.

One person begins by drawing a charade card and acting out the verse or message on it. This can be done one word at a time or in a way that captures the whole message. Either way the actor cannot talk. The rest of the team or participants call out their guesses. Give them a minute or so to guess correctly, and then tell them the message.

❏ **Reproducible 2A**

❏ scissors

Choose another actor and repeat the process. Continue through the rest of the cards.

Ask: Were some messages easier to guess than others? If so, why? How hard do you think it would be to explain the Gospel message to people whose way of life you did not understand?

Say: John and Charles Wesley went to Georgia to carry the Gospel to the colonists. Charles Wesley served as secretary to the colony's founder, General James Oglethorpe. John Wesley hoped to be a missionary to the native tribes, but instead was assigned as the parish preacher for the colonists. The Anglican priest from London did not understand the ways of the people, and the people living in the new frontier did not understand John Wesley. They rebelled at his insistence on strict rules of behavior. John had his own ideas about what it meant to live as a Christian and he did not take time to get to know the people and understand their needs. The result was a communication disaster that sent John and Charles fleeing back to England.

Barefoot Pencil Pass   Time: 5 minutes

Everyone needs to be barefoot.

Sit in a circle of chairs. Put a pencil on the floor in front of one tween.

The challenge is to see how quickly the group can pass the pencil around the circle using just their toes. The first person picks up the pencil with her toes and drops it in front of the next person, who continues the process. If anyone has too much difficulty, just pick up the pencil and pass it to the next person.

When they are done, read "The Barefoot Preacher" (What Is a United Methodist?—pp. 11-12).

Ask: How do you think the children would have responded if John Wesley had gone to their class and lectured them about treating the poor children with respect? Why do you think his method was so effective? Have you ever learned a lesson by watching someone's behavior?

STUFF—BAREFOOT PENCIL PASS:

❏ **What Is a United Methodist?**

❏ a pencil

☐ **Bible**

☐ **Reproducible 2B**

☐ **What Is a United
Methodist?**

☐ **pencils**

✳ **COOL OPTION:**
Write the words to
Ephesians 2:8 on a markerboard.
Have tweens read the verse aloud
together. Erase the last word.
Repeat reading the entire verse.
Erase the next to the last word.
Repeat reading the entire verse.
Continue erasing one word at a
time from the end of the Scripture
until tweens can recite Scripture
from memory.

The Heart of the Matter Time: 20–25 minutes

Hand out pencils and "Two Dramatic Stories"
(Reproducible 2B—p. 20).

Read "A Storm at Sea." Give tweens a few minutes to
respond to the questions. Invite tweens who wish to do so
to share their responses.

Ask a volunteer to read Joshua 1:9. Read "A Heart-warming
Experience." Again give the tweens a few minutes to write
and share their responses.

**Say: This was a life-changing experience for John Wesley.
Even though he had been a Christian all of his life, he had
never felt this personal assurance of God's love. Wesley came
to a new understanding that we do not have to earn our
salvation; it is a gift from God. Wesley turned to his Moravian
friends when he was going through this time of
discouragement and spiritual crisis.**

Ask tweens if they have someone they can go to for
guidance when they are going through a difficult time or
facing a tough decision.

Invite any who are willing to share their responses to the
questions.

Read Ephesians 2:8. Have the tweens repeat it after you,
phrase by phrase, to memorize the verse.

John Wesley kept journals throughout his life. Read
together Wesley's own account of his Aldersgate experience
(**What Is a United Methodist?**—p. 13).

**Say: Wesley's Aldersgate experience was an important
milestone in his faith journey, but it was not the beginning,
and it was not the end. Being a Christian means opening
ourselves to God's love and guidance every day as we seek to
grow closer to God through Jesus Christ. The road of faith is
not always smooth. We may have times when, like John
Wesley, we do not feel the assurance of God's love. In those
times, dig into the Bible for reminders that God is always with
us.**

Going to the People Time: 15–20 minutes

Say: In John Wesley's time, as today, many people were working on Sunday mornings. Worship in the Church of England was a very formal affair. Many of the poor and working common folk did not feel comfortable coming into the churches. George Whitefield solved that problem by preaching out in the fields where the people were. He encouraged John Wesley to do the same. Wesley was so deeply connected to the formal worship of the Church of England that he found it hard at first to imagine field preaching as acceptable. Then he remembered Jesus' model of teaching not only in the synagogues, but out among the people.

Wesley's first sermon given in the fields was heard by about three thousand people. That sounds great to us, but a bishop of the Church of England banned Wesley from the pulpit for preaching in the field. Still, Wesley remained an Anglican all of his life. He simply defied the bishop's orders and preached where he felt God was calling him to preach.

Ask: If you were going to take the message of Christ to where the people are in your town, where would that be?

Say: Write a message you would give to a group who is not in the church to help them know God's love.

Invite any who wish to do so to share their message with the group.

STUFF—GOING TO THE PEOPLE:

☐ paper

☐ pencils

Three General Rules Time: 10 minutes

Say: Many people became Christians because of the preaching of John Wesley. Wesley realized that it was not enough for people to say, "I believe in Jesus." In order to grow in faith and live as Christ calls us to live, we need to study the Bible and have the guidance of mature Christians. Many of these new Christians could not read, so one important ministry of the Methodists was education. They tutored and started schools. Wesley organized the converts into Societies led by trained lay people (not ordained ministers). The Societies met weekly to study the Bible, pray, collect offerings for the poor, and be sent out to serve. The Society members held each other accountable for living the Christian life by answering the questions of self-examination.

STUFF—THREE GENERAL RULES:

☐ **What Is a United Methodist?**

☐ pencils

Wesley laid out three general rules for the Societies. See if your tweens can break the code (**What Is a United Methodist?**—p. 15) to discover these rules.

Ask: How would your school be different if everyone practiced these rules? How would our church be different? How would you be different?

WORSHIP

Time: 2 minutes

Ask a volunteer to read Ephesians 2:8.

Close with prayer, asking God to help you live in peace with your neighbor and to stay close to God through Jesus Christ.

TAKE IT FURTHER

Faith Stories Time: 20 minutes

Read Romans 1:16.

Say: Paul wrote these words to the church in Rome. Paul experienced persecution throughout his ministry because he would not stop telling the good news of Jesus Christ. Eventually, Paul was arrested, taken to Rome, and put to death because he would not deny Christ and stop witnessing to his faith. In some parts of the world today people still risk imprisonment and death for declaring their faith in Jesus. Though we do not risk those consequences here, many Christians are reluctant to talk about their faith.

Ask: Why do you think that is so? Have you ever talked to anyone outside of church about Jesus? What do you think would happen if you started talking to people at school about your faith?

Invite your guests to share their faith story. Open up the conversation, allowing the tweens to ask questions and share their own stories if they wish.

STUFF—WORSHIP:

❑ **Bible**

STUFF—FAITH STORIES:

❑ **Bible**

❑ guests

❊ **COOL OPTION:** Divide tweens into three groups. Write the words of each of today's Scriptures (see page 13) on a separate index card. Give each group one of the cards and tell them to think of an unusual way to deliver their message.

Examples: Write it and fold it into a paper airplane, write it in code, have a parade while chanting the words, make a poster. Encourage creativity.

Reproducible 2A
HOLY CHARADES CARDS

▲ Jesus loves you.

▲ Believe in Jesus and you will be saved.

▲ Repent of your sins.

▲ The Bible is God's Word for you.

▲ Jesus called twelve disciples.

▲ Live in peace with one another.

▲ Jesus is the Son of God.

▲ Love one another as God has loved you.

▲ Jesus died on the cross for your sins.

▲ Ask, and it will be given you; search, and you will find; knock, and the door will be opened for you.

Reproducible 2B
TWO DRAMATIC STORIES

A Storm at Sea

John and Charles Wesley set sail in October 1735 for the colony of Georgia. Among the passengers was a group of Moravians, a persecuted group of German Christians. John became friends with them. One night there was a terrible storm. The waves crashed against the ship so fiercely it sounded as if the ship would crack. The ship tossed about wildly. It was a frightening time, and many were ill. Though many of the passengers were panicked, the Moravians remained calm. They gathered together for prayer and assured the others they could trust God to care for them. Through the stormy times in Georgia, John remembered the Moravians and their total trust in God's loving care.

If you have ever been through a bad storm, describe how you felt.

Have you ever been through a stormy situation in your life?

Was there anyone you looked to as a model for how to deal with the tough situation?

Did you feel God's presence with you?

Even when we don't feel the assurance of God's presence, God is there.

"Be strong and courageous; do not be frightened or dismayed, for the LORD your God is with you wherever you go." Joshua 1:9

A Heart-warming Experience

After his failed mission to Georgia, John Wesley went back to England a discouraged man. He felt like he had let God down. Life seemed so dark, it was hard to see the light of God's love. John remembered the strong faith he'd witnessed in the Moravians during the storm at sea. He got connected with a group of Moravians in London. One evening he went to one of their meetings at a house on Aldersgate Street. As someone was reading aloud from a commentary about God's love, something amazing happened. John later wrote in his journal, "I felt my heart strangely warmed." In that moment he felt the assurance of God's love for him and knew that whatever failures he might have, whatever troubles might come his way, there was nothing that could keep him from God's love and forgiveness.

Wesley's life was changed when he felt this new assurance of God's forgiving grace. Have you every had a life-changing encounter with God or do you know someone who has?

A UNITED METHODIST IS . .

THE WORLD IS MY PARISH

THE MAIN IDEA

American Methodism grew in response to Christ's call to "go and make disciples of all nations."

THE GOALS

Tweens will
- learn about the beginnings of the Methodist Church in America.
- reflect on strengths and weaknesses in church policies.
- recognize that members of the church are responsible for reaching out and welcoming new persons, without restrictions.

THE BIBLE

Matthew 28:19–20, Philippians 1:20–21, Acts 10:34-35

THE PLAN

Get Ready

John and Charles Wesley were clergy in the Church of England, also known as the Anglican Church. In America that church is known as the Episcopal Church. Today we will see how the Methodist movement within the Church of England became a separate church in America. In opposition to the authorities in the Church of England, John Wesley followed what his heart and Scripture told him

STUFF TO COLLECT:

- [ ] **Bibles**
- [ ] chairs
- [ ] two slips of paper
- [ ] marker
- [ ] pencils
- [ ] scissors
- [ ] bulletin board or long roll of colored paper; markers
- [ ] construction paper and glue
- [ ] **Reproducible 3A, p. 27**
- [ ] **Reproducible 3B, p. 28**
- [ ] **Reproducible 3C, p. 55**
- [ ] **Reproducible 3D, p. 56**
- [ ] **Reproducible 3E, p. 57**
- [ ] **What Is a United Methodist?**

For cool ❄ *options*:

- [ ] **What Is a United Methodist?**
- [ ] pencils

STUFF TO DO:

1. Use two slips of paper and a marker to make two bookmarks. Each should say "Matthew 28:19-20."
2. Make photocopies of Reproducibles 3A and 3B and cut cards apart.
3. Make photocopies of Reproducibles 3C, 3D, and 3E.

 **LOOK AHEAD:**
An optional activity for next week is learning about your church's history. If you'd like to explore that with your tweens, take time this week to gather resources and invite in persons who are longtime members of your church and leaders who know some of the church's history.

STUFF—PONY EXPRESS RACE:

- ☐ **Bibles**
- ☐ chairs
- ☐ two slips of paper
- ☐ marker

⬤ ⬤ ⬤ ⬤ ⬤

⬤

⬤ ⬤ ⬤ ⬤ ⬤

by taking to the fields and factories to preach the good news. When reprimanded for this action, John replied, "The world is my parish." With this vision it was inevitable that he would send Methodist preachers to the American colonies.

In today's world of instant communication, tweens may need to be reminded of the challenges Wesley faced in leading the Methodist Societies in America from across the sea. Though Wesley's writings provided the framework, leaders were needed "on the ground" to see that the converts were nurtured in the faith, new preachers were trained, and circuit riders were assigned and sent out into the towns and countryside. Only ordained clergy had authority to offer the sacraments of Holy Communion and baptism. Given a choice between obeying Anglican church law or obeying Christ's call to "make disciples of all nations," Wesley chose Christ. He took upon himself a bishop's role and ordained Thomas Coke as superintendent for the church in America with full authority to ordain others. That action set off the chain of events that led to the establishment of the Methodist Episcopal Church.

Like today, Christians had to make choices about how to live their faith. Some of those choices helped bring about changes in society like better education and health care for the poor. Other choices led to continued oppression of marginalized persons. Challenge tweens to think of ways your church can reach out to marginalized groups in your community.

GET STARTED

Pony Express Race Time: 5 minutes

Place one chair in the middle of an open area. Set up two rows of folding chairs, one on each side, facing the center. You will need a chair for each person. Each row should be about five to six feet back from the center chair (see sidebar).

Write the Bible reference "Matthew 28:19-20" on two slips of paper. Put one of these bookmarks in each Bible and set the Bibles on the first chair in each of the rows.

Say: Circuit riders were preachers who rode from one church community to another, often traveling hundreds of miles a month on horseback.

The person in the far left seat of each row will be the circuit rider and run with the Bible around the center chair and back to the end of the row. Meanwhile, everyone in the row will stand up and shift one chair to the left, creating a vacant seat at the end for the circuit rider. The circuit rider passes the Bible up the row to the person in the first chair, who becomes the new circuit rider. That person takes the Bible and circles the middle chair and back to the end of the row. The game continues in the same way until the Bible is back in the hands of the original circuit rider. That person stands, opens the Bible to Matthew 28:19-20, and reads those verses aloud.

Famous Words Time: 5 minutes

Say: John Wesley was a preacher in England. Preaching happened from the pulpit on Sunday morning. It was thought undignified to stand on a street corner and preach.

Ask: What would you think if your pastor stood on a street corner or in the mall parking lot preaching?

Say: John Wesley believed that he was called to take the gospel to the people. He was careful not to preach in fields during the time of regular Sunday worship. Still, when Wesley began preaching in the fields in Bristol, England, the bishop of Bristol objected.

Ask tweens to discover what Wesley said to the bishop (*What Is a United Methodist?*—p. 16).

Say: Wesley responded, "The world is my parish." Those words would become the rallying cry for Methodist preachers, lay and ordained, as they went out into the world to share the gospel by word and action.

DIG IN

Key People Time: 15–20 minutes

Copy and cut apart all the biography and "Who Am I?" cards on pages 27-28 (**Reproducibles 3A and 3B**).

Choose four readers and give each person one of the "Early Days in America: Biography" cards (**Reproducible 3A**) to read aloud.

TIP: Tweens will understand directions better if given one at a time.

STUFF—FAMOUS WORDS:

❑ **What Is a United Methodist?**

❑ pencils

STUFF—KEY PEOPLE:

❑ **Bible**

❑ **Reproducible 3A**

❑ **Reproducible 3B**

❑ scissors

TIP: Place the biography cards in the middle of a table or post them on the wall so that tweens can refer to them and not have to rely totally on memory.

Then randomly choose one of the "Early Days in America: Who Am I?" cards. After it is read, ask the group to vote on which of the four people they think it refers to. Don't give the answer until all four "Who Am I?" cards have been read and voted on. (Answers are on page 62.)

Say: According to the law of the Church of England only a bishop could ordain a person into ministry. John Wesley was not a bishop; he was simply an ordained minister. The preachers in America kept writing John asking for more ordained ministers to spread the gospel and take the sacraments of baptism and Holy Communion to the outposts of the new land. There were many among the new converts who were gifted and called to preach, but they lacked official church authority to offer the sacraments. John Wesley did not want to defy the Anglican bishop, but he also could not ignore the call for ordained ministers. He convinced himself that as supervisor of the itinerant ministers in America, he had authority to lay hands on Thomas Coke to ordain him as superintendent of the American Methodists. Coke then went to America and laid hands on Francis Asbury, ordaining him as a bishop as well. The two of them then had the authority to ordain lay preachers as full clergy.

Continue with "Key People" by asking for four volunteers to read the biography cards for "Breaking Barriers" (Reproducible 3B–p. 28). Then read the "Who Am I?" card (also on p. 28) one at a time. After each is read, have the tweens vote on which person they think is being described.

Ask: What challenges do you think the Methodist preachers faced in the American colonies that they did not face in England? (There were great distances from one place to the next, a very small number of ordained clergy, and no formal church structure.) **What opportunities do you think they had that they did not have in England? (**New converts who felt God calling them to spread the gospel were encouraged to preach and teach the Word; the American Methodists could form their own church structure.)

Read Philippians 1:20–21.

Say: Paul wrote these words to the church in Philippi. These words also reflect the faith of the circuit riders. They risked their lives by pushing themselves constantly to reach more and more people with the gospel. Francis Asbury traveled five to six thousand miles a year on horseback through all kinds of weather and regardless of his personal health. He risked

ensure and conflict by speaking out against the drinking of alcohol and the practice of slavery. Though Asbury did receive a small salary, he kept only what he needed to survive and gave the rest to those needier than himself.

Ask: Are there people today who are as committed to serving Christ as these early circuit riders? Why do you think we do not see more people like this?

The Church Fails a People   Time: 15 minutes

Review the biography of Richard Allen (Reproducible 3B—p. 28). Hand out copies of "A History of Hope and Shame" (Reproducibles 3C and 3D—pp. 55-56).

Ask for volunteers to read each of the sections on the reproducibles.

Ask: Are you surprised by the church's treatment of African Americans? Why or why not?

Invite tweens to imagine a history in which the Methodist Church stayed true to the teachings of Jesus by devotedly working for equal rights for all persons and never practicing segregation or discrimination within the church.

Ask: What difference might the church have made in the history of our country? What difference might the church have made in the lives of people of all races? Do you think the church can influence the policies and practices of society?

Knowing You   Time: 15 minutes

Hand out the pencils and copies of "The Perfect Gift" (Reproducible 3E—p. 57).

Say: Read the descriptions of each person. Then match each person with the perfect gift. Be ready to explain why you chose the gift you did.

Read each description and ask for a show of hands to indicate how many chose a particular gift. Then ask them to explain why they chose that gift.

After they have given their explanations, read the full descriptions of the individuals (see sidebar, p. 26).

STUFF—THE CHURCH FAILS A PEOPLE:

❏ Reproducible 3B

❏ Reproducible 3C

❏ Reproducible 3D

STUFF—KNOWING YOU:

❏ Reproducible 3E

❏ pencils

✳ COOL OPTION: John Wesley's belief in the equality of all persons was based on the Scriptures. Have tweens break the code (What Is a United Methodist?—p. 18) to discover what Peter said in Acts 10:34-35 about the value of all people.

Isaiah Jones is a 6'2" athletic African American man in his early twenties. He is a dancer with a small ballet company and dreams of becoming a principal dancer with a major ballet. He would love tickets to a ballet.

Maria Mendoza, at 5'4", stands proud of her Mexican heritage. She is a leading scorer on her sixth-grade basketball team and hopes to someday play on a college team as her father did. She would love the basketball shoes.

Kaitlyn Richardson is a recently retired senior citizen. She was part of the engineering team that designed the Mars rover. She is always interested in new technology, so she would love the latest techie gadget.

Simon Smith—At 6'5", this Caucasian man has to duck when going through doorways on his way to class. He loves the carpentry classes he is taking at Trades & Technology School and hopes to someday own a furniture refinishing shop. An antique rocking chair would be the perfect gift.

Sarah Leibowitz is a girl of German heritage who works in a coffee shop in New York City. When not at the coffee shop, she uses her creative gift to make quilts. She would highly value a handmade Amish quilt.

STUFF—WORSHIP:

- [ ] nothing

STUFF—BULLETIN BOARD:

- [ ] **Reproducibles 3A and 3B**

- [ ] bulletin board or long roll of colored paper and markers

- [ ] scissors

- [ ] construction paper and glue

Say: Even when we are trying to be open-minded, it is easy to jump to false conclusions.

Ask: Have you ever made wrong assumptions about someone?

Say: When this is taken to the extreme, we can make assumptions about whole groups of people. This can have tragic and long-lasting results.

Ask: Think about our congregation. Are there a variety of ages, races, and socioeconomic groups? What population is being overlooked by the church in your community? (Overlooked populations might include single parents, children and teens whose parents aren't involved in church, the homeless, or persons struggling with substance abuse.)

Think of ways the church might minister to these persons and invite them to join in ministry with you.

WORSHIP

Time: 1 minute

Close with prayer, thanking God for all those who have gone before, faithfully living out God's call.

TAKE IT FURTHER

Share Bulletin Board Time: 20-30 minutes

Work together to create a bulletin board or mural about Methodism. Divide the space into three areas: "Early Methodism," "Woven Together," and "This We Believe." Work this week on Early Methodism. Over the next two weeks you will add to the mural. Brainstorm what persons or events should be included in the section on Early Methodism. You will want to go back to Sessions 1 and 2 for information on John and Charles Wesley.

Let the congregation know about the project so they can learn from you. You might even want to include question cards with answers on the back as part of the display.

BIOGRAPHY AND WHO AM I? CARDS

The Early Days in America: Biography
Robert Strawbridge

I'm an Irish immigrant farmer who answered God's call to preach in the American colonies. I'm a lay person, just like you. Even though the Church of England and Methodist rules say only ordained clergy can offer the sacraments of Holy Communion and baptism, I do it anyway for the sake of the people.

The Early Days in America: Who Am I?

I organized the first Methodist Society in the American colonies and was the first American circuit rider for the Methodist Societies.
Who am I?

The Early Days in America: Biography
Francis Asbury

I was appointed by John Wesley to take the gospel to the American colonies. At the Christmas Conference in 1784, I was elected to share with Coke the office of joint superintendent of the Methodist Episcopal Church. As one of Methodism's most dedicated circuit riders, I traveled around 5,000 a year on horseback.

The Early Days in America: Who Am I?

I'm known as the "father of American Methodism" and was the only Methodist preacher from Britain who continued preaching in America through the Revolutionary War.
Who am I?

The Early Days in America: Biography
Thomas Coke

I was ordained by John Wesley as a superintendent (later called bishop) with authority to go to America and ordain Asbury as a fellow superintendent. We then had authority to ordain those serving as lay ministers in America, giving them the right to offer the sacraments.

The Early Days in America: Who Am I?

My ordination was done without Charles Wesley's knowledge, and Charles was furious when he found out! (John knew that Charles would not approve of this action because, under the rules of the Church of England, John did not have the authority to ordain others.) *Who am I?*

The Early Days in America: Biography
Thomas Rankin

I am a Scottish-born preacher and convert to Methodism. I was sent to America in 1773 to make sure the preachers were following the discipline set down by Wesley for Methodist Societies.

The Early Days in America: Who Am I?

I returned to England in 1778, during the Revolutionary War, because of my loyalty to the crown. I was a close friend of John Wesley and was with him when he died.
Who am I?

Reproducible 3B

BIOGRAPHY AND WHO AM I? CARDS

Breaking Barriers: Biography
Richard Allen

I was born into slavery, but was able to buy my own freedom. I was converted to Christianity by a circuit rider and became a traveling preacher myself. I started the African Methodist Episcopal Church after a group of blacks were forcibly removed from St. George's Methodist Episcopal Church in Philadelphia as we knelt in prayer.

Breaking Barriers: Who Am I?

After starting my own church, I successfully sued the Methodist Episcopal Church over my church's right to remain independent.
Who am I?

Breaking Barriers: Biography
John Stewart

I'm a man of mixed race who was converted at a Methodist camp meeting. Later I answered God's call to take the gospel to the Wyandot Indians of Ohio.

Breaking Barriers: Who Am I?

The ministry I started became the first church-wide mission of the Methodist Episcopal Church.
Who am I?

Breaking Barriers: Biography
Amanda Berry Smith

I was born into slavery in 1837, but my father later purchased my freedom. I was a very successful traveling evangelist who brought many people to Christ. My preaching drew large audiences in both the North and South, and even white audiences came to hear me speak.

Breaking Barriers: Who Am I?

I am a published author. I traveled as a missionary to Africa and established a home for black orphans.
Who am I?

Breaking Barriers: Biography
Barbara Heck

I immigrated to America with a small group of Irish Methodists. I encouraged my cousin Philip Embury to start a Methodist Society. After my husband and I left America during the Revolutionary War, I helped establish Methodist Societies in Canada.

Breaking Barriers: Who Am I?

I was alarmed at the drinking and card playing of so called Christians and believed the Methodist Societies could help people lead disciplined lives in the way of Christ.
Who am I?

A UNITED METHODIST IS . . .

WOVEN TOGETHER

THE MAIN IDEA

The United Methodist Church is woven together from different denominations who share Wesleyan roots and a desire to be the church together.

THE GOALS

Tweens will
• learn about the beginnings of The Evangelical United Brethren Church.
• see how The United Methodist Church was formed from different strands.
• think about what the Scriptures say about believers getting along.

THE BIBLE

Ephesians 4:1-5

THE PLAN

Get Ready

"Why can't everybody just get along?" Your tweens have probably heard that said a few times at home or at school or even on church outings. Throughout the history of The United Methodist Church there have been times when God may have wanted to shout, "Why can't everybody just get along!" There have been arguments that led to splits in the

❏ **Bibles**
❏ pencils
❏ scissors
❏ index cards
❏ crayons or markers
❏ any resources gathered about your church's history
❏ guests
❏ paper
❏ bulletin board or long roll of paper
❏ construction paper and glue
❏ **Reproducible 4A, p. 35**
❏ **Reproducible 4B, p. 36**
❏ **What Is a United Methodist?**

For cool ❉ *options*:

❏ nothing

STUFF TO DO:

1. Make photocopies of Reproducible 4A and cut cards apart.
2. Make photocopies of Reproducible 4B.

☀👁 **LOOK AHEAD**
Next week you will be discussing the sacraments. You may want to invite your pastor to celebrate Holy Communion with the class.

STUFF—A TANGLED WEB:

☐ nothing

church over how the church is organized. There have been more fundamental differences over who belongs in the church and who may be given authority. As in our own families, some arguments get worked out and some do not.

This session is about differences, but also about ways the church has set aside differences to unite as a stronger church. Knowing about our roots can help us understand who we are. Knowing our church history can help us understand why The United Methodist Church has certain practices even today, such as itinerant preachers who are moved to new churches as the bishop and cabinet see fit.

Last week tweens were introduced to Richard Allen, an African American slave who bought his own freedom and became a Methodist preacher. Today they will learn more about how the question of equality impacted the church and those they would serve. This history lesson is important to remember as the church continues to struggle with who belongs and how the church is to live out its mission to make disciples for Jesus Christ.

Tweens understand conflict. They know what it is to have someone swear to "never speak to them again." The words of John Wesley are helpful in reminding us to pick our battles carefully and to focus on what unites us rather than on what divides us. Wesley wrote these wise words in 1750: "May we not be of one heart, though we are not of one opinion?" As your tweens work and discuss together, help them find ways to be of one heart.

GET STARTED

A Tangled Web Time: 10 minutes

Six to eight tweens stand in a circle. Each tween takes the hand of persons across the circle. The challenge is to untangle the knot without letting go of hands. Allow no more than ten minutes for them to work on this. Usually the knot can be untangled completely.

Ask: How did it feel when you were all knotted up? What things helped the group get untangled?

Say: Today we will be talking about the church connection. People in a church are connected by their faith in Christ.

A church community is also connected by the history they share as an individual church and as part of a denomination. A strong church is also connected by its vision for the future, for how the members can grow in their own faith and how they can make disciples and serve the world.

All in the Family Time: 10 minutes

Give tweens about five minutes to complete the "Family History" questions (**What Is a United Methodist?—p. 19**) about the family in which they live. Assure them that many people know very little about their family history, but to do the best they can. Then ask them to share their stories in groups of three.

Say: **We can learn something about ourselves by knowing more about the families from which we come. Today we are going to be learning about our faith family tree with the roots of United Methodism.**

DIG IN

Evangelical United Brethren Time: 15 minutes

Like last week, play "Key People" (see pp. 23-25). This week's questions will help tweens learn about United Methodist roots in the Evangelical and United Brethren churches.

Copy and cut apart the "German Connection" biography and "Who Am I?" cards (**Reproducible 4A, p. 35**). Choose four people to come in front of the group. Give each person one of the biography cards to read aloud.

Then randomly choose one of the "Who Am I?" cards. After it is read, ask the class to vote on which of the four people they think it refers to. Don't give the answer until all four "Who Am I?" cards have been read and voted on.

Say: **The people you learned about today had a strong connection with John Wesley and the Methodist Societies. When they organized into churches, they based their structure and laws on those of the Methodists.**

STUFF—ALL IN THE FAMILY:

❑ **What Is a United Methodist?**

❑ pencils

STUFF—EVANGELICAL UNITED BRETHREN:

❑ **Reproducible 4A**
❑ scissors
❑ index cards
❑ pencils

 TIP: If you have time, play the game again with last week's cards as a review.

Ask: Why do you think they did not just join with the Methodists? (German was their only or primary language.)

Say: Like John Wesley, Philip William Otterbein had an experience of great spiritual renewal. Also like Wesley, Otterbein was already a Christian and a preacher when he had this experience. Otterbein came to America as a minister for the German Reformed Church. He was a very popular preacher and soon had the second largest Reformed congregation in America. His "heart-warming" experience came after a particularly moving sermon. He was approached after church by a man who felt overwhelmed by his sin and wanted Otterbein to explain to him about God's grace. Otterbein was shocked to realize he could not answer the man. He decided not to preach again until he had the assurance of God's forgiving love and his own salvation. Through prayer he did receive that assurance and began to preach again with a new vigor and passion.

Say: Whether you are a new Christian or an ordained minister, it is natural to have times of questioning your faith. Those times of questioning can drive us to seek God in ways that strengthen and enrich our faith.

Give each tween an index card. Ask each to write on the card one question they have about faith. Instruct them not to sign the cards, so that no one else will know who wrote the question.

Gather the cards. Look through them. If there are any you can answer, do so. For the others tell them you don't know the answers, but you're willing to try and find some answers.

Share the questions with your pastor this week. Share the pastor's answers next week or ask the pastor to come to the session and answer the questions.

The Family Tree Time: 15–20 minutes

Hand out "The History of United Methodism" diagram (**Reproducible 4B—p. 36**) and set out the crayons or markers.

Give tweens time to look over the diagram and mark it as directed.

Review together the completed diagram.

TIP: Remember to follow through with answering questions to the best of your ability in the next session.

If a complete answer is difficult or the idea is too abstract for a concrete thinker to understand, it is perfectly alright to explain that we don't have answers to everything. Some things we must take on faith.

STUFF—THE FAMILY TREE:

❏ Reproducible 4B

❏ What Is a United Methodist?

❏ pencils

❏ crayons or markers

Say: Churches are made up of people, and by God's design we are each unique. It is natural that in churches, as in other parts of life, people have differences of opinion.

Ask: Can you think of any situation in which it would be a good thing for a group to break off from a church to start their own church?

Say: There were other denominations that broke off from The Methodist Episcopal Church at different times. Among the earliest were the African Methodist Episcopal Church and The African Methodist Episcopal Zion Church, which left because of discrimination. Other African Americans stayed in The Methodist Church. They remained in the church and worked for change.

What About Me? Time: 10–15 minutes

Say: John Wesley had some things to say about differences between members of his Methodist Societies. He talked quite a bit about it in a sermon he titled "Catholic Spirit." We think of *catholic* as referring to a particular denomination, but the word means "universal." So in "Catholic Spirit" Wesley is speaking about things that bring us together as Christians.

Have the tweens discover what John Wesley said about differences between Christians by completing the crossword puzzle "Wise Words of Wesley" (**What Is a United Methodist?**—pp. 20-21).

Say: Remember that Wesley lived and wrote in the 1700's, so his use of language is a little different from ours today.

Work together to put this in modern language.

Say: Sometimes in the middle of a conflict in the church, people may wish they were back in the New Testament church when everyone believed the same things and worked together. The truth is that people are people in every age, and there were plenty of conflicts in the early church. Much of Paul's letters were about conflicts in churches.

Invite a volunteer to read Ephesians 4:1-5 to hear what Paul had to say to the church about getting along with one another.

Ask: Do you know of any conflicts in our church? What holds our church together?

STUFF—WHAT ABOUT ME?:

❑ Bible

❑ What Is a United Methodist?

❑ pencils

Possible modern wordings:

We all think differently about things, but we all can love. All the children of God can agree on this.

OR

All God's children can agree to disagree and still love one another.

❑ **Bible**

❑ any resources gathered about your church's history
❑ guests
❑ pencils and paper

❑ **Reproducibles 4A and 4B**

❑ bulletin board or long roll of colored paper

❑ markers

❑ scissors

❑ construction paper and glue

TIP: You may wish to add a photocopy of the diagram to the bulletin board.

WORSHIP
Time: 2 minutes

Ask a volunteer to read Ephesians 4:4-5.

Say a prayer for your church and for love, understanding, and, tolerance in your congregation.

TAKE IT FURTHER

My Church's History Time: 20 minutes

Let tweens look through any historic church pictures or documents you have brought in. Talk about ways the church has changed.

Invite the special guests to tell about the early history of your church. Ask them how the church building has changed over the years, if at all. What changes do they see in the style of worship? Has the focus of mission and outreach changed over the years?

Ask tweens to imagine what the church might be like 25 years from now. If you have time, they might draw a literal picture that captures words and symbols that show what they think the church will be like in the future.

Add to Bulletin Board Time: 15–20 minutes

Work on the next section of the bulletin board or mural about Methodism. Work this week on the section "Woven Together." Tweens will want to look back at the biography questions and the diagram of the history of the church.

Add information and pictures about your own church.

Reproducible 4A

BIOGRAPHY AND WHO AM I? CARDS

The German Connection: Biography
Phillip William Otterbein
I said "Wir sind Bruder" (we are brothers) to the evangelical German preacher I heard at a revival at Long's barn in Pennsylvania. We later formed the United Brethren Church.

The German Connection: Who Am I?

Though not a Methodist, I was invited to join in laying hands on Francis Asbury at his ordination as joint superintendent (bishop). *Who am I?*

The German Connection: Biography
Martin Boehm
I am a Mennonite preacher from Pennsylvania who believes that personal holiness is more important than church structure and creeds. I speak and preach in German, the language spoken by many of the people in this area.

The German Connection: Who Am I?

Though I was not a member of the English-speaking Methodists, I identified with their emphasis on grace and provided a plot of ground on which they could build a chapel.
Who am I?

The German Connection: Biography
Jacob Albright
I started my own German-speaking church in 1803 based on the Bible and structured after the Methodist Episcopal Church.

The German Connection: Who Am I?

After the sudden death of three of my children, I met Christ through a Methodist preacher and joined a Methodist class.
Who am I?

The German Connection: Biography
John Dreisbach
I was converted to Christianity at age 17 and was licensed to preach a year later by Jacob Albright. In 1814, I was elected the first presiding elder in the Evangelical Association. Fluent in German and English, I am a gifted writer and hymn writer.

The German Connection: Who Am I?

Francis Asbury tried unsuccessfully to convert me to Methodism.
Who am I?

Reproducible 4B

THE HISTORY OF UNITED METHODISM

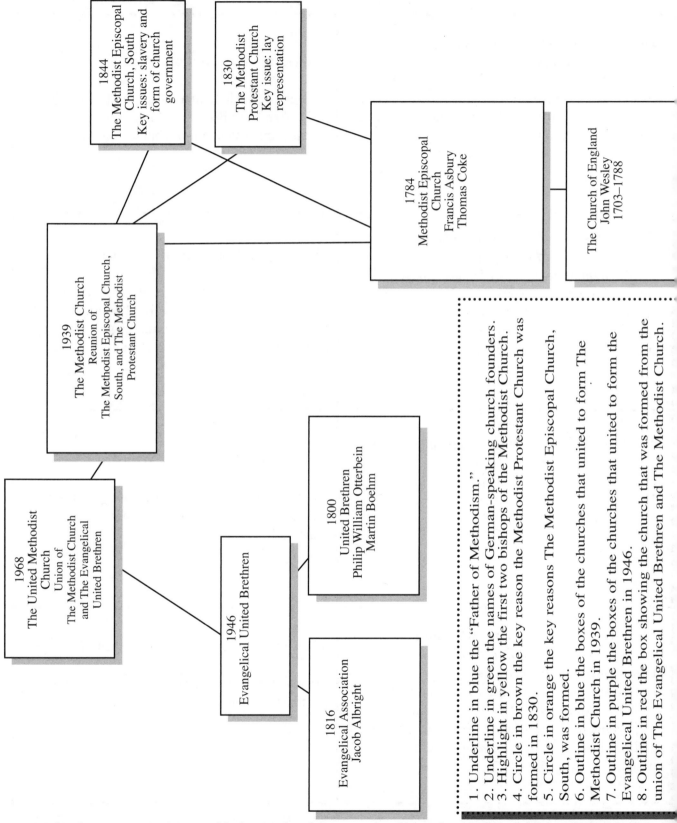

1844
The Methodist Episcopal Church, South
Key issues: slavery and form of church government

1830
The Methodist Protestant Church
Key issue: lay representation

1784
Methodist Episcopal Church
Francis Asbury
Thomas Coke

The Church of England
John Wesley
1703–1788

1939
The Methodist Church
Reunion of
The Methodist Episcopal Church, South, and The Methodist Protestant Church

1968
The United Methodist Church
Union of
The Methodist Church and The Evangelical United Brethren

1946
Evangelical United Brethren

1800
United Brethren
Philip William Otterbein
Martin Boehm

1816
Evangelical Association
Jacob Albright

1. Underline in blue the "Father of Methodism."
2. Underline in green the names of German-speaking church founders.
3. Highlight in yellow the first two bishops of the Methodist Church.
4. Circle in brown the key reason the Methodist Protestant Church was formed in 1830.
5. Circle in orange the key reasons The Methodist Episcopal Church, South, was formed.
6. Outline in blue the boxes of the churches that united to form The Methodist Church in 1939.
7. Outline in purple the boxes of the churches that united to form the Evangelical United Brethren in 1946.
8. Outline in red the box showing the church that was formed from the union of The Evangelical United Brethren and The Methodist Church.

A UNITED METHODIST IS . . .

AMAZING GRACE

THE MAIN IDEA

Belief in and dependence on God's grace is central to United Methodists.

THE GOALS

Tweens will
- be able to define the three kinds of grace as defined by John Wesley.
- recognize and affirm the ways God's grace prepares and enables us to live the Christian life.
- name the two sacraments in United Methodism.
- experience confession and thanksgiving.

THE BIBLE

Matthew 28:19-20a, Mark 9:1-11, Luke 22:19-20, Ephesians 4:4-6

THE PLAN

Get Ready

Warning: This session is full of lots of big ideas that mature Christians still struggle to grasp. But by God's grace we are not required to pass a test to become Christians, just to trust and believe. That is the good news you can share with your tweens. Encourage tweens to ask questions and share your own with them. Be familiar with the material, but also

- ❑ **Bibles**
- ❑ markerboard or newsprint
- ❑ markers
- ❑ pencils
- ❑ sticky notes
- ❑ bulletin board or long roll of paper
- ❑ construction paper and glue
- ❑ scissors
- ❑ pastor
- ❑ communion elements
- ❑ **Reproducible 5A, p. 43**
- ❑ **Reproducible 5B, p. 44**
- ❑ **Reproducible 5C, p. 58**
- ❑ **What Is a United Methodist?**

For cool ❄ *options*:

- ❑ church bulletins
- ❑ pencils
- ❑ **The United Methodist Hymnal**
- ❑ **What Is a United Methodist?**

STUFF TO DO:

1. Make photocopies of Reproducibles 5A, 5B, and 5C.

be willing to say, "I don't know." Sometimes "I don't know" can be followed by, "but I'll try to find out." Sometimes you just need to acknowledge that some things will always be a mystery in this life.

God's grace is the heart of United Methodist belief. Grace is God's wondrous act of love that reaches out to us even before we know there is a God and continues to work within us all our lives. John Wesley's heart-warming experience on Aldersgate Street was a personal encounter with God's grace. While Wesley continued to stress the importance of living a disciplined Christian life, he also had the assurance that such a life is made possible by God's sustaining grace.

The sacraments are visible signs of God's grace. United Methodists, like other Protestants, believe there are two sacraments, baptism and Holy Communion. Some of your tweens may have been baptized as infants. Others may not have been baptized. Baptism is an outward sign that we are children of God and part of the body of Christ. Depending on the practices of your church, your tweens may not all have participated in communion. If time and circumstances allow, you may want to arrange for a minister to celebrate communion with the class. Whether or not you experience communion together, the tweens will have an opportunity to make a private confession to God and to offer their thanksgivings. Confession and thanksgiving are two key parts of communion. Let this session be a time to affirm and celebrate God's gift of grace.

GET STARTED

Faith Builders Time: 10 minutes

As tweens arrive, ask them to write on a markerboard or newsprint names of persons who have helped them grow in faith and knowledge of God. Next to the name they should write the person's role in their life, such as "parent," "teacher," "neighbor," "youth counselor," and so forth. Write your responses also.

When finished, look at all of the names. Is there a wide variety of roles represented? Are there certain roles that come up repeatedly? Did anyone name others in the room? If so, how does it feel to be named as a faith builder?

TIP: After the "Faith Builders" exercise, take time to answer any of last week's faith questions that still remain unanswered.

That Grace Word Time: 5–10 minutes

On the markerboard or newsprint write "un" followed by eleven blanks for the word *unexplainable.*

Say: Today we are talking about grace. What do you think of when you hear the word *grace*?

Since grace has several different meanings, from a prayer at the table, to mercy, to a gift from God, tweens may offer a variety of responses.

Down one side of the board or newsprint count down from ten: 10, 9, 8, 7, 6, 5, 4, 3, 2, 1.

Say: You will have ten chances to guess the missing letters. The word begins with "un" and describes God's grace.

Go around the room giving each person a chance to guess a letter. At any time, if someone thinks he or she knows the word, that person may offer a guess. Repeat the process for the words *undeserved* and *unending*.

DIG IN

Grace That Saves Time: 20–25 minutes

Give everyone a Bible and a copy of "Three Kinds of Grace" **(Reproducible 5A—p. 43).**

Say: A key mark of United Methodists is the belief that God's grace is for all. John Wesley experienced God's grace at a meeting on Aldersgate Street. In his journal he wrote, "I felt my heart strangely warmed. I felt I did trust in Christ, Christ alone for salvation, and an assurance was given me that he had taken away my sins, even mine, and saved me from the law of sin and death." Remember that grace is the free gift of God's love. John Wesley spoke of three kinds of grace: prevenient grace, justifying grace, and sanctifying grace.

Read through the descriptions of grace together. Then ask tweens to discover the answers to the questions by unscrambling the words. If they can't figure out the words, have them look up the designated Scriptures. Go over the answers together (see p. 63).

STUFF—THAT GRACE WORD:

- [ ] markerboard or newsprint
- [ ] marker

TIP: If they do not guess the words, ask them to complete "Pick a Vowel" **(What Is a United Methodist?—p. 22).** This will help them finish the words.

STUFF—GRACE THAT SAVES:

- [ ] **Bibles**
- [ ] **Reproducible 5A**
- [ ] pencils

Divide into three groups. Assign each group one of the grace sections of The United Methodist Hymnal. Tell them to go through their section and find and mark hymns written by Charles Wesley. The hymn writer is listed at the bottom left of the page. Read through the words of at least one hymn from each section.

STUFF—SIGNS OF GRACE:

- ❏ Bibles

- ❏ What Is a United Methodist?

- ❏ Reproducible 5B

- ❏ pencils

Ask: What does grace tell you about the nature of God? (God is loving. God's love is for all. God is forgiving. God helps us do right.)

Say: Prevenient grace helps us admit that we have fallen short of God's will for us. Because God gave us free will, we have to choose whether or not to follow Jesus. When we repent of our sins, God forgives us and offers us the gift of new life through Jesus Christ.

Say: Being a Christian doesn't mean we're perfect. But it does mean that if we stay tuned into God through prayer, Bible reading, worship, and Christian fellowship, God will help us to better live the way Jesus taught us to live.

Say: Charles Wesley helped take the message of God's grace to the people through hymns. Many of the words he wrote were set to familiar tunes. Even today The United Methodist Hymnal includes sections on prevenient grace, justifying grace, and sanctifying grace. In each of these you will find many of Charles Wesley's hymns.

Signs of Grace Time: 15 minutes

Christians participate together in special encounters with Christ that we call sacraments.

Ask: Do you know what sacraments are observed by United Methodists? (baptism and Holy Communion)

Say: A sacrament is a sign of God's grace. United Methodists, along with most other Protestant denominations, believe that sacraments are practices experienced by Jesus and commanded by him. The two sacraments observed by United Methodists are baptism and Holy Communion.

Ask tweens if they have participated in Holy Communion. Who has been baptized?

Learn more about baptism (**"What Is a United Methodist?" pp. 24-25**). Give tweens a minute to read through and check the statements they think all Christians believe about baptism and the statements they think United Methodists believe about baptism. Then read each statement aloud, asking the tweens to stand up if it is one of the statements they checked. Go over the correct answers (see p. 63). Hand out "Two Sacraments" (**Reproducible 5B—p. 44**).

Say: Since sacraments are something experienced by and commanded by Jesus, we can read about them in the Bible. Use your Bibles to complete the passages about baptism and Holy Communion.

Ask for volunteers to read the completed statements aloud.

Ask: Which method of baptism is most commonly practiced in our church? Have you seen or experienced baptism by immersion?

Ask a volunteer to read Ephesians 4:4-6.

Ask: Do you think United Methodists would recognize a baptism that was performed in another denomination? (yes) **If a person wanted to be baptized again as a reaffirmation of his or her faith, do you think that would be appropriate?** (No, there is "one baptism." Baptism is a sign of God's action, and God's work is always sufficient.)

Go over what United Methodists believe about Holy Communion (**Reproducible 5B—p. 44**).

Say: Sacraments are holy mysteries. Though we do not fully understand them, we can fully experience God in Christ through them.

WORSHIP

Confession and Thanksgiving Time: 15 minutes

Ask: What do you think are the requirements for receiving communion in The United Methodist Church? (none except the desire to respond honestly to the invitation)

Hand out the Liturgy for Holy Communion (**Reproducible 5C—p. 58**).

Read the invitation.

Ask: What requirements are given in the invitation? (love Jesus, repent of sin, seek to live in peace with one another)

Read the confession aloud together.

Say: In The United Methodist Church you do not have to

COOL OPTION: Let tweens solve "Three Names, One Sacrament" (**"What Is a United Methodist?"—p. 26**).

STUFF—WORSHIP:

❑ **Bibles**

❑ **Reproducible 5C**

❑ sticky notes

❑ pencils

COOL OPTION: If your tweens are comfortable with each other, have them form prayer partners with the person next to them. Have each pair move away from others so they can have a quieter space for sharing. Ask them to turn to their partners and share one thing they would like their partners to pray about for them.

STUFF—TAKE IT FURTHER: WHAT WE BELIEVE:

- ❏ bulletin board or long roll of paper

- ❏ construction paper and glue

- ❏ scissors

- ❏ markers

- ❏ pencils

STUFF—TAKE IT FURTHER: RECEIVE HOLY COMMUNION:

- ❏ pastor

- ❏ communion elements

confess to a priest; you confess directly to God. Part of the confession is done together as a whole church. This is followed by a time of silent confession.

Invite tweens to take a few moments in silence to write on a sticky note their personal confession to God. These are just between them and God and will not be shared.

Say: Since the early church, one of the things the gathered community did was sing hymns. If you have hymnals, sing or read aloud the words to "I Am the Church" or "Forward Through the Ages." Otherwise, sing a praise song the group knows.

Let a volunteer read Ephesians 4:4-6.

Say: One of the important things we do as the body of Christ is to pray for one another and for the world.

Begin with a prayer for the group and then allow a moment for a time of silent prayer. Close with the Lord's Prayer.

TAKE IT FURTHER

What We Believe Time: 15–20 minutes

Add to the bulletin board or mural that you began in Session 3. Create symbols that represent United Methodist beliefs about grace and the sacraments. Cut out words to make a collage or write definitions or questions to add to the display.

Receive Holy Communion Time: 10–15 minutes

Invite your pastor to come and celebrate the sacrament of Holy Communion with the class. You may want to do this in your classroom setting or move to the sanctuary for this special worship time.

A UNITED METHODIST IS . . .

Reproducible 5A
THREE KINDS OF GRACE

United Methodist belief and practice emphasize God's grace.
John Wesley spoke of three kinds of grace.

Prevenient Grace

The grace that comes before we are even aware of God. Prevenient grace calls us to repent of our sins. Prevenient grace is like a light at the end of a tunnel. It shines to show us the way.

When does God's love for you begin?
MFOR EHT MMNOET OUY
ERA CCEIONVDE

_____ ____ _____ ____

____ _____

Need help?
Read Psalm 139:13-14.

To whom is God good and for whom does God have compassion?
    LAL

_____

Need help?
Read Psalm 145:9.

Is God's gift of grace dependent on our actions?
    ON

_____

Need help?
Read Romans 5:8.

Justifying Grace

The grace that saves us. No one, by their own actions, can be right with God. We all fall short of perfection.

Justifying grace puts us into a right relationship with God.

Just like "justified margins" set the type straight down the right and left margins of a page, justifying grace is grace through which our sins are forgiven and we are set straight with God.

Are we saved by our efforts to be good?
    ON   ____

What is our part in salvation?
    AFIHT   _____
Need help?
Read Ephesians 2:8.

Who can receive the gift of salvation?
LAL OHW VAHE FHTIA

_____ _____ _____ _____

Need help?
Read Romans 1:16.

Justification, or saving grace, is a gift of God through whom?
HSIRCT SSEJU

_____ _____

Need help?
Read Romans 3:23-25.

Sanctifying Grace

The grace that helps us be more loving toward God and creation. We are saved by faith, but we respond to salvation by trying to be obedient to God.

We are called to live in the way of Christ and are able to do that through the Holy Spirit. Like cartoon transformers that transform into "super heroes," we are transformed by grace and provided with power through the Holy Spirit.

If God lives in us, how will that love be made known?
NI HTTUR DAN NICTOA

___ _____ _____ _____

Need help? Read I John 3:17-18.

Becoming more like Christ is possible, by God's grace, because through Christ everything has
CMBOEE WEN

_____ _____.

Need help?
Read 2 Corinthians 5:17.

Having been made right with God, we are transformed into God's image. Who or what makes this transformation possible?
EHT PSRITI FO EHT RLDO.

_____ _____ ___ _____ ___.

Need help?
Read 2 Corinthians 3:18.

Reproducible 5B
TWO SACRAMENTS

A sacrament is a sign of God's grace. United Methodists, along with most other Protestant denominations, believe that sacraments are practices experienced by Jesus and commanded by him. The two sacraments observed by United Methodists are baptism and Holy Communion.

▶ *Baptism* ◀

Jesus experienced baptism. He was baptized by _____. At the time of his baptism a _____ descended as a sign that the Holy Spirit was with him. (Mark 9:1-11)

Jesus commanded his disciples to practice baptism. He told them:"[Go] and make disciples of all nations, _____ them in the name of the _____ and of the _____ and of the _____, and teaching them to obey everything that I have commanded you." (Matthew 28:19-20a)

United Methodists recognize and practice:

Baptism by sprinkling
The minister dips a hand in the water and literally sprinkles it onto the head of the one being baptized. Sprinkling symbolizes cleansing from sin and being set apart for service to God.

Baptism by pouring
In baptism by pouring, a shell or other object is used to scoop up water which is poured over the head of the candidate. Again the use of water is a reminder that in baptism we are cleansed of our sin. Pouring the water is a reminder of the outpouring of the Holy Spirit.

Baptism by immersion
Immersion requires a special pool or access to a river or lake. The baptismal candidate and minister stand in the water. The person being baptized lies back onto the minister's arms and is dipped under the water. The act of going completely under the water and back up demonstrates the belief that in baptism we die to sin and rise again into new life in Christ.

▶ *Holy Communion* ◀

When Jesus observed the Last Supper with his disciples, he commanded believers to practice this sacrament as a way to remember him. The Gospel of Luke tells us: "Then he took a _____ of _____, and when he had given _____, he _____ it and gave it to them, saying, "This is my _____, which is given for you. Do this in _____ of me." And he did the same with the _____ after supper, saying, "This _____ that is poured out for you is the new _____ in my _____. (Luke 22: 19-20)

United Methodists believe Holy Communion is a "means of grace" that is a way through which we may come to know the saving grace of Jesus Christ. It is a time of remembering the life of Jesus and a way of looking forward to Christ's final victory. The bread and wine (or juice) are not physically changed into the body and blood of Christ, but believers are transformed by the real presence of Christ through the sacrament.

A UNITED METHODIST IS . . .

OPEN HEARTS, OPEN MINDS, OPEN DOORS

THE MAIN IDEA

United Methodists believe God still speaks and calls us to serve the least and the lost.

THE GOALS

Tweens will
- be able to name and apply the four parts of the Wesleyan quadrilateral.
- become familiar with the administrative structure of The United Methodist Church.
- experience prayer.
- reflect on ways Jesus reached out to the least and the lost.

THE BIBLE

Psalm 25:4-5, Matthew 22:36-39, Luke 4:18, John 1:1-5, James 2:14-17

THE PLAN

Get Ready

Part of understanding Methodism is understanding how the church is connected. Though the church connection helps the church function smoothly administratively, it is also an important way in which the church lives as the body of Christ. The United Methodist Church is able to serve those in need around the world more effectively because the

PREPARE YOUR SESSION

STUFF TO COLLECT:

- ☐ pencils
- ☐ markerboard or newsprint
- ☐ markers
- ☐ **Reproducible 6A, p. 51**
- ☐ **Reproducible 6B, p. 52**
- ☐ **Reproducible 6C, p. 59**
- ☐ **Reproducible 6D, p. 60**
- ☐ **Reproducible 6E, p. 61**
- ☐ **What Is a United Methodist?**

For cool ❄ *options*:

- ☐ nothing

STUFF TO DO:

1. Make photocopies of Reproducibles 6A, 6B, 6C, 6D, and 6E.

churches work together. The church at work in the world is an important part of what it means to be United Methodist. The church says to each member, "You are a valued child of God who has gifts to share." Tweens want to know that they can make a difference. Help them understand what it means to be a disciple and discover how they can better serve God and others.

With our gifts from God comes a responsibility to use them for God's glory in service to others. The slogan of The United Methodist Church is "open hearts, open minds, open doors." Jesus calls us to care for the least and the lost. John Wesley took this call seriously. He required members of Methodist Societies to care for those in need with their time, their money, and their service. Wesley insisted that we need to get personally involved.

Tweens will be introduced to how United Methodists do theology. Wesley used four sources for knowing God and how God wants us to live. The most important source is Scripture. Wesley also knew God through experience. The tradition of the church that has helped us understand such things as the Trinity is also an important way we know God. We also use our God-given power to reason. United Methodists believe that the Bible is constantly revealing and that God continues to speak in the world. If we are to hear God, we must keep an open mind. Reflect back on what it means to be a United Methodist.

GET STARTED

Living the Faith Time: 10 minutes

As tweens arrive, tell them to write on markerboard or newsprint what they think of when they hear the word *disciple*.

Read through the list of words.

Say: Sometimes people just think of the twelve disciples that Jesus called. All who follow Jesus are disciples. Being a disciple means following the example of your master. How we live out our faith as disciples of Jesus Christ is very important.

Say: Jesus said there are two basic laws. The first is to love God with all our heart and strength and mind. The second is to love our neighbor as ourselves (Matthew 22:36-39). How we

STUFF—LIVING THE FAITH:

- ❏ **Bibles**

- ❏ **Reproducible 6A**

- ❏ pencils

- ❏ markerboard or newsprint

- ❏ markers

live is the fruit of our faith. As we live by these two commandments we are drawn closer to Christ.

Have tweens complete "Discipleship Guide" (**Reproducible 6A—p. 51**).

Ask: How did you do? Remember John Wesley would say we are going on to perfection by God's grace. That doesn't mean we are there yet! Go back and put a star next to three things you would like to work on this year.

Ask a volunteer to read James 2:14-17 aloud.

Say: James is saying that our faith will be shown by our works.

We're Connected Time: 15 minutes

Say: The United Methodist Church is a connectional system. Each church is connected to the rest of the church body through layers of administration which allow the church to work more effectively to carry out its mission. Our connectional system also ensures that the churches follow the discipline (laws) of The United Methodist Church.

Turn to "The Connected Church" (**What Is a United Methodist?—pp. 28-29**) to see how The United Methodist Church structure connects.

Say: When you think of the church you probably think of this local church. But let's start instead with the whole United Methodist Church.

Hand out "The United Methodist Church" (**Reproducible 6B—p. 52**) and read through it together. Answer the questions at the bottom. (Answers are on page 63.)

Say: It may seem like a lot of structure, but the connectional system reminds us that we are not Christian alone. We are the body of Christ. In all of these layers of church government are people. When the people of The United Methodist Church gather at Annual Conference, it is, in many ways, a family reunion. People greet with joy people they may not have seen for a year. They struggle together, with all of their differences, to find how God calls them to witness for Christ in the world.

STUFF—WE'RE CONNECTED:

❏ **What Is a United Methodist?**

❏ **Reproducible 6B**

❏ pencils

❏ **What Is a United
   Methodist?**

❏ **Reproducible 6C**

**Statements for Four Wesleyan
Corners:**

1. Jesus is the son of God.
2. Jesus is my savior.
3. The church is the body of
   Christ.
4. God is three in one being.
5. The world is so awesome it
   must be the result of a Creator
   God.
6. God is with me when I'm
   afraid.
7. God wants me to forgive others
   as I have been forgiven.

DIG IN

Living the Faith Time: 10 minutes

**Say: John Wesley talked about four sources for knowing God
and what it means to be a Christian.**

Read "The Wesleyan Way of Knowing" (**What Is a United
Methodist?—p. 27**).

Ask: What is the first and most important source? (Scripture)
**What do you think of when you hear the word *tradition*?
What do you think of when you hear the word *experience*?
When you hear the word *reason*?**

**Say: When John Wesley used the words *tradition*, *experience*,
and *reason*, he had very specific meanings in mind.**

Hand out "Four Ways to Truth" (**Reproducible 6c—p. 59**).
Read the descriptions of Scripture, tradition, experience,
and reason.

Four Wesleyan Corners:
Point to four corners in the room and call one "Scripture,"
one "tradition," one "experience," and one "reason."

**Say: I will read a series of statements. After each one, go and
stand in the corner that best represents what would help you
have that belief.**

Tweens will probably respond differently to the statements.
For some people, their greatest understanding of a truth
may come from experience, for another the Bible, and so
forth. We can give thanks that we have different means
through which to know God.

**Say: Sometimes Christians focus so much on the small stuff
that they miss the big message God is trying to give us. Being
a disciple of Jesus Christ is about more than what we believe;
it is about living our beliefs.**

Read John 1:1-5.

Ask: Who is the Word John is talking about? (Jesus)

**Say: We talk about the Bible as the Word of God, but Jesus is
also the Word in human form. When you are confused by**

something in the Bible, one way to better understand is by thinking about how Jesus, the Word, would respond. Look in other places in the Bible to find what Jesus did or said, and think about your own experiences of Christ and those of Christians through the ages. When you do those things, you are using the Wesleyan quadrilateral to help you know God. United Methodists believe that the Bible is constantly revealing God's word to us and that God continues to speak in the world.

The Least and the Lost Time: 15–20 minutes

Read Luke 4:18.

Ask: This is Jesus' declaration of his mission. What does Jesus say he came to do?

Say: In carrying out his mission Jesus frequently came into conflict with religious and political leaders.

Hand out "The Least of These" (Reproducible 6D—p. 60). Have half of the group read the first two Scriptures and the other half read the second two Scriptures, filling in the chart.

Ask each group to summarize what happened in each of their readings and tell how they completed the chart. (Answers are on page 63.)

Ask: From these stories, who do you think Jesus would say is welcome in his kingdom? Who would he say is welcome in the church? Did Jesus meet the least and the lost in the Temple?

Say: Jesus went out among the people. Some people came up to Jesus when he was passing by to ask him to heal them. Other times Jesus called out to people and invited them to come to him.

Read the paragraph about John Wesley on the bottom of the handout.

Ask: Why do you think some of the people just wanted to send money to those in need? Why did John Wesley insist they actually visit the sick, the poor, and those in prison?

Brainstorm ways your church is in ministry to the least and the lost, and list these on the markerboard or newsprint. Circle projects in which members are personally involved.

STUFF—THE LEAST AND THE LOST:

- ❏ Bibles
- ❏ Reproducible 6D
- ❏ What Is a United Methodist?
- ❏ pencils
- ❏ markerboard or newsprint
- ❏ markers

STUFF—WORSHIP:

☐ **Bibles**

☐ **Reproducible 6E**

☐ pencils and markers

For "Reach Out":

Design a label that includes the name of your church, the church address, worship times, and a word of welcome.

Cut a hole in the bags about two inches from the top so that the bag can be hung on a door knob.

Have the tweens write a personal note on the three-by-five-inch cards, something like: Hi! I'm _____, one of the youth at _____ Church. I have a great time with the youth there and my parents like their Sunday School class. We'd love to see you in worship!

Put a welcome label on the outside of each bag. Inside place an informational flyer, welcome card, and some of the candies. Go around the neighborhood, hanging a bag on each door.

STUFF—TAKING IT FURTHER:

☐ informational flyers or church brochures

☐ wrapped candies

☐ white or brown lunch bags

☐ index cards

☐ pens and markers

☐ label sheets

☐ access to a computer

Read a famous saying of John Wesley's, "Do All the Good You Can" (**What Is a United Methodist?—p. 5**).

Say: The slogan of The United Methodist Church is "open hearts, open minds, open doors."

Ask: Based on what you have learned about United Methodism, do you think this is a good slogan?

WORSHIP

Knowing God Time: 15 minutes

Say: We know God from the Scriptures, our faith experiences, the tradition of the church, and through our reasoning. Think about ways you know God. Maybe there are certain images of God that you have found in the Bible. Maybe you've had an experience of feeling God's love, forgiveness, or peace. Maybe there are traditions from church teaching or worship that have helped you know God. Maybe there are things you have learned in Sunday School. Use words, phrases, or symbols to describe some of the ways you know God.

Give tweens "Knowing God" (**Reproducible 6E—p. 61**) and ten minutes to work. Invite any who are willing to share to do so.

Read Psalm 25:4-5.

Close with prayer. Ask God's help to know God better and to serve God through Jesus Christ.

TAKE IT FURTHER

Reach Out Time: 20-40 minutes

Make welcome bags to take around to homes in the church neighborhood (see sidebar to the left above).

You will need permission slips from parents for tweens to go around the neighborhood. You will also need an adult to accompany each group of tweens.

Reproducible 6A
DISCIPLESHIP CHECKUP

How is your discipleship?
Are these practices that you usually follow, sometimes follow, or never follow?

	Usually	Sometimes	Never
I help people in need through donations or service.			
I treat others as I would like to be treated.			
I pray for those in need.			
I thank God in good times and in bad.			
I trust in God and do not get anxious.			
I am not ashamed of the gospel, and I tell others about Jesus.			
I love and pray for those who say or do hurtful things to me.			
I forgive others as God forgives me.			
I use my gifts for God's glory.			
I celebrate the gifts of others and am not jealous of them.			
I am patient and kind.			
I do not demand my own way.			

Reproducible 6B
THE UNITED METHODIST CHURCH

▲ Local Church
The pastor is the leader of the church, but the lay members have an important voice in all decisions as they serve on and chair committees, teach classes, and volunteer for and lead mission teams. The pastor and laity are accountable to the bishop through the person of the district superintendent. Lay and clergy members are elected by each church to attend Annual Conference.

▲ Districts
Each Annual Conference is divided into districts, along geographic lines. The district superintendent oversees all of the churches in the district, helping provide resources to train leaders and carry out the ministry of the church.

▲ Annual Conference
Annual Conference refers to both a yearly gathering of church members and clergy and the name given to a geographic division of churches. Though some states have more than one Annual Conference and some Annual Conferences are made up of more than one state, most Annual Conferences are divided along state lines. The Annual Conference is presided over by a bishop. A primary responsibility of the bishop, assisted by the district superintendents, is to appoint the clergy to all of the churches in the Conference. As in Wesley's time, United Methodist ministers "itinerate." That means they are moved from church to church as appointed by the bishop.

▲ Jurisdictional Conference
This group also meets every four years and is made up of delegates from the various Annual Conferences within a particular geographic region. Its primary responsibility is electing and assigning bishops to lead the Annual Conferences.

▲ General Conference
General Conference is the only body of The United Methodist Church that can change church law. General Conference meets every four years. There are an equal number of lay and clergy delegates to General Conference, elected by the members of all the Annual Conferences.

● **Who is the leader of an Annual Conference?**
● **How often does General Conference meet?**
● **Which conference elects bishops?**
● **Who assigns pastors to local churches?**

A UNITED METHODIST IS . . .

ADDITIONAL REPRODUCIBLES

Reproducible 1C
ASKING THE TOUGH QUESTIONS

The questions listed here are similar to ones Wesley used in small groups.
Ask yourself these questions. Take them home and post them where you can ask them regularly.

Wesley's Questions for Self-Examination

1. Am I giving the impression that I am better than I really am; in other words, am I a hypocrite?
2. Do I pass a secret someone trusted me with?
3. Can I be trusted?
4. Am I a slave to dress, friends, or habits?
5. Am I self-conscious, do I feel sorry for myself or make excuses for myself?
6. Did the Bible live in me today?
7. Do I give the Bible time to speak to me every day?
8. Am I enjoying prayer?
9. When did I last speak to someone else of my faith?
10. Do I pray about the money I spend?
11. Do I get to bed on time and get up on time?
12. Do I disobey God in anything?
13. Do I insist upon doing something even though my conscience tells me not to?
14. Is there something I've given up on?
15. Am I jealous, impure, critical, irritable, touchy, or distrustful?
16. How do I spend my spare time?
17. Am I proud?
18. Is there anyone whom I fear, dislike, disown, criticize, resent or ignore?
    If so, what am I doing about it?
19. Do I grumble or complain constantly? (In other words, do I whine?)
20. Is Christ real to me?

☞ My friends, watch out! Don't let evil thoughts or doubts make any of you turn from the living God. You must encourage one another each day. And you must keep on while there is still a time that can be called "today." If you don't, then sin may fool some of you and make you stubborn. We were sure about Christ when we first became his people. So let's hold tightly to our faith until the end. **Hebrews 3:12-14 (CEV)**

A UNITED METHODIST IS . . .

Reproducible 3C
A HISTORY OF HOPE AND SHAME

Acceptance

John Wesley was a passionate opponent of slavery. He would not accept the argument that slavery was acceptable because it was lawful. In "Thoughts Upon Slavery" Wesley wrote, "Notwithstanding ten thousand laws, right is right and wrong is wrong." Wesley called the institution of slavery inhuman. He wrote, "The African is God's child as much as the Englishman." Wesley's teachings on the equality of all persons were lived out in the American colonies at first. African slaves and freed men who were gifted and called to preach were given authority to do so. Among the early black preachers were Harry Hosier and Richard Allen. Though whites were sometimes drawn in by the dynamic preaching, black preachers were usually sent out to preach to black people. St. George's Methodist Episcopal Church in Philadelphia was one place where blacks and whites worshiped together.

Rejection

The number of black participants at St. George's grew under Richard Allen's leadership in the black community. When the church leaders asked the congregation to raise money to add a balcony to the growing church, the blacks participated in the effort. Imagine the shock and pain when the balcony was built and they were told that was where they had to sit from then on. Still, they continued to worship at St. George's. Then a final blow was delivered. Two black worshippers were forcibly removed from the church as they knelt at the front in prayer. Richard Allen marched out with them.

John Wesley

Richard Allen

Art: Robert S. Jones, © 1997 Cokesbury: *J.W. & Company*, pp. 207, 221.

New Life

Richard Allen started his own black Methodist church. This church later became the African Methodist Episcopal Church. The AME denomination continues today, carrying on the Wesleyan tradition. Although the primary ministry is to the African American community, the AME Church has always welcomed whites as members, refusing to practice the discrimination they experienced. The AME Church has over two million members in churches around the world, including North America, South America, Africa, and Europe.

In 1844 the Methodist Episcopal Church split over the issue of slavery. An even harder truth is that the split remained after the Civil War. Almost one hundred years later in 1939, when the Methodist Episcopal Church, the Methodist Episcopal Church, South, and the Methodist Protestant Church reunited, one condition of the union was that the black churches be governed by their own bishop in a separate Central Jurisdiction. Through the efforts of African American and white leaders, the Central Jurisdiction was eliminated in 1968, when The Methodist Church joined with The Evangelical United Brethren Church to form The United Methodist Church.

Think About It

Imagine a history in which the Methodist Church stayed true to the teachings of Jesus by devotedly working for equal rights for all persons and never practicing segregation or discrimination within the church.

▲ What difference might the church have made in the history of America?

▲ What difference might the church have made in the lives of people of all races?

▲ Do you think the church can influence the policies and practices of society?

Reproducible 3E
THE PERFECT GIFT

Read the description of each person, and then match that person
with the perfect gift from the column on the right.

People	Gifts
● **Isaiah Jones** is a 6'2" athletic African American man in his early twenties.	▲ tickets to the ballet
● **Maria Mendoza**, at 5'4", stands proud of her Mexican heritage.	▲ an antique rocking chair
● **Kaitlyn Richardson** is a recently retired senior citizen.	▲ the latest techie gadget
● **Simon Smith**, at 6'5", this Caucasian man has to duck when going through doorways on his way to class.	▲ a handmade Amish quilt
● **Sarah Leibowitz** a 20-something girl of German heritage who works in a coffee shop in New York City.	▲ basketball shoes

Reproducible 5C
A UNITED METHODIST LITURGY FOR THE SACRAMENT OF HOLY COMMUNION

**Below you will find a reprint of a portion of the liturgy for Holy Communion.
In your church you may use this or a variation of it.**

United Methodists practice "open communion." All are welcome at the table who respond to the invitation. You do not have to be a member of the church. You do not have to be a certain age. The service of communion begins with the invitation and is followed by a statement of confession.

▲ INVITATION

Christ our Lord invites to his table all who love him,
    who earnestly repent of their sin
    and seek to live in peace with one another.
Therefore, let us confess our sin before God and one another.

▲ CONFESSION AND PARDON

**Merciful God,
we confess that we have not loved you with our whole heart.
We have failed to be an obedient church. We have not done your will,
we have broken your law,
we have rebelled against your love,
we have not loved our neighbors,
and we have not heard the cry of the needy.
Forgive us, we pray.
Free us for joyful obedience,
through Jesus Christ our Lord. Amen.**

All pray in silence.

Leader to the people:

Hear the good news:
    Christ died for us while we were yet sinners;
    that proves God's love toward us.
In the name of Jesus Christ, you are forgiven!

[Following confession, there may be a time to pass the peace of Christ in greeting to one another.

Before Jesus offered the bread and cup to his disciples, he gave thanks to God.

Before we receive communion there is a time of thanksgiving to remember God's gracious acts, particularly Jesus' words at the Last Supper and his sacrifice for us.

We remember what Christ did for us in the past and ask that he continue to be at work in us, transforming us in this world in preparation for the time we feast with Christ in his heavenly kingdom.]

By your Spirit make us one with Christ,
    one with each other,
    and one in ministry to all the world,
until Christ comes in final victory,
    and we feast at his heavenly banquet.

(From "A Service of Word and Table V," The United Methodist Hymnal, pp. 12-15.)

Art: Randy Wollenmann, © 2008 Cokesbury, *Rock Solid: Tweens in Transition Annual Resource Pak 2008-09*, p. 35.

     A UNITED METHODIST IS . . .

Reproducible 6C
FOUR WAYS TO TRUTH

United Methodists believe that our faith is "grounded in Scripture, informed by Christian tradition, enlivened in experience, and tested by reason."
(From The Book of Discipline of The United Methodist Church)

▲ Scripture

The Bible is the foundation for our faith. It is the primary way we know God and provides us with everything we need to know for salvation. So why do we need anything else?

The writers of the Bible were inspired by God, but because their world was so different from ours, some things can be confusing if we don't use our minds (reason) and church tradition and the experience of ourselves and other Christians to reflect on their writings.

▲ Tradition

This doesn't refer to tradition as the way we've always done things. The insights given to Christians through the ages make up tradition. An example of a belief that comes from Scripture and tradition is our understanding of the Trinity. The word *trinity* is not used in the Bible. By studying Scripture, Christians have come to understand that God is One but is experienced as God the Father, the Son, and the Holy Spirit.

▲ Experience

Paul never saw Jesus in the flesh, but he speaks of meeting Jesus on the road to Damascus. John Wesley was assured of God's forgiveness when he felt his heart "strangely warmed" while at a prayer meeting. The experiences of other believers like these, as well as our own experiences of God, help shape our faith.

▲ Reason

God created us with the ability to learn new things. We apply our knowledge as we read Scripture. Few Christians insist women cover their heads in prayer, even though Paul instructs women to do this in the Bible. We know from historians that this was part of the culture of the time, so we are able to say that it was important for women in Paul's time, but not today.

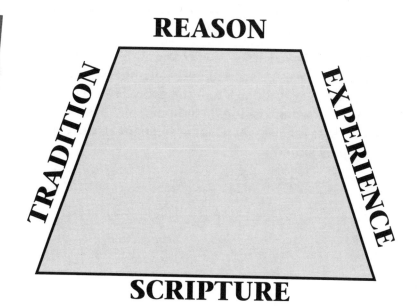

REASON

TRADITION

EXPERIENCE

SCRIPTURE

Reproducible 6D
THE LEAST OF THESE

**"Truly I tell you, just as you did it to one of the least of these who
are members of my family, you did it to me." Matthew 25:40**

Over and over again Jesus shows us that we are to care for those in need and to reach out to those whom
society would cast aside. Read one or more of the Scriptures listed and complete the chart by answering
the questions.

Scripture	Who is the least?	How did others respond?	How did Jesus respond?
Matthew 9:9-13			
Luke 7:36-50			
Luke 19:1-10			
John 8:2-11			

**John Wesley followed Jesus' model and went out among the people to minister to their physical and
spiritual needs. Wesley insisted to the members of the Methodist Societies that the Scriptures
command us to visit the sick and the poor. Not everyone liked that idea. They protested, saying,
"But is there need of visiting them in person? May we not relieve them at a distance?" Wesley
responded that it is only by looking someone in the eye that one part of the world can know what
the other part suffers.**

(From Wesley's Sermon 50, "The Use of Money," and Sermon 98, "On Visiting the Sick")

A UNITED METHODIST IS . . .

Reproducible 6E
FOUR WAYS TO TRUTH

United Methodists believe we can know God through Scripture, tradition, experience, and reason. With symbols, words, or phrases, express ways you know God through these four sources.

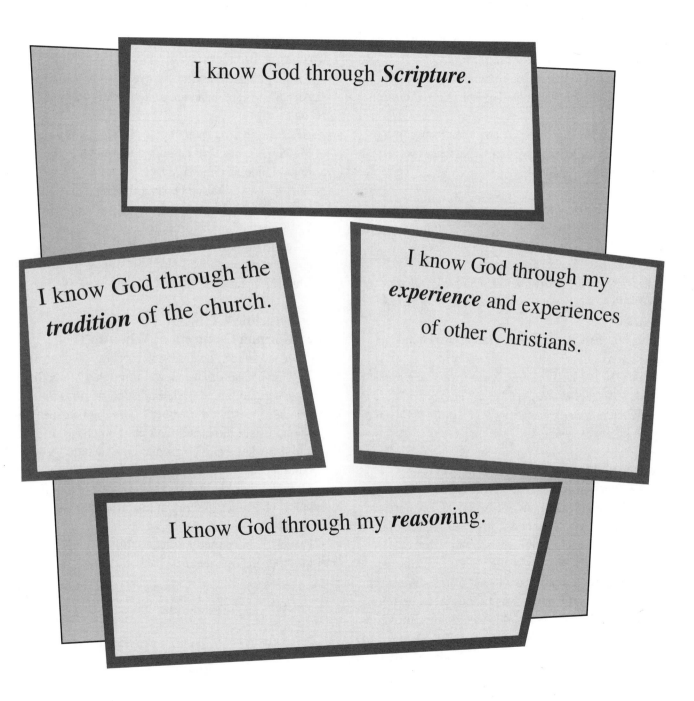

I know God through *Scripture*.

I know God through the *tradition* of the church.

I know God through my *experience* and experiences of other Christians.

I know God through my *reason*ing.

Answers

Reproducible 1B, p. 12
Rate Your Bible Literacy
- Name the four Gospels: *Matthew, Mark, Luke,* and *John*
- What book of the Bible tells a story of the creation of the world? *Genesis*
- What are the first nine words of the 23rd Psalm? *The Lord is my shepherd, I shall not want.*
- Who heard God speaking in a burning bush? *Moses*
- Who baptized Jesus in the River Jordan? *John (the Baptist)*
- Jesus told his disciples, "If any want to become my followers, let them deny themselves and take up their *cross* and follow me."

- Match these people with the event:

Paul—*Met Jesus when he was blinded on the Damascus Road*

Peter—*Denied Jesus three times*

Judas—*Betrayed Jesus for thirty pieces of silver*

Noah—*Was shown the rainbow as a sign of God's covenant*

Jacob—*Name was changed to Israel; was father of twelve sons*

Joseph—*Sold by his brothers into slavery in Egypt*

Moses—*He told Pharaoh, "Let my people go."*

Isaiah—*A prophet who told of a Messiah who would suffer for the people.*

Reproducible 3A, p. 27
Early Days in America: Who Am I?
- I'm known as the "father of American Methodism" and was the only Methodist preacher from Britain who continued preaching in America through the Revolutionary War. *Asbury*
- My ordination was done without Charles Wesley's knowledge and Charles was furious when he found out! (John knew that Charles would not approve of this action because under the rules of the Church of England John did not have the authority to ordain others.) *Coke*
- I organized the first Methodist Society in the American colonies and was the first circuit rider for the Methodist Societies. *Strawbridge*
- I returned to England in 1778, during the Revolutionary War, because of my loyalty to the crown. I was a close friend of John Wesley's and was with him when he died. *Rankin*

Reproducible 3B, p. 28
Breaking Barriers: Who Am I?
- I am a published author. I traveled as a missionary to Africa and established a home for black orphans. *Smith*
- After starting my own church, I successfully sued the Methodist Episcopal Church over my church's right to remain independent. *Allen*
- The ministry I started became the first church-wide mission of the Methodist Episcopal Church. *Stewart*
- I was alarmed at the drinking and card playing of so called Christians and believed the Methodist Societies could help people lead disciplined lives in the way of Christ. *Heck*

Reproducible 4A, p. 35
The German Connection: Who Am I?
- After the sudden death of three of my children, I experienced spiritual renewal through a Methodist preacher and joined a Methodist class. *Albright*
- Though I was not a member of the English-speaking Methodists, I identified with their emphasis on grace and provided a plot of ground on which they could build a chapel. *Boehm*
- Though not a Methodist, I was invited to join in laying hands on Francis Asbury at his ordination as Bishop. *Otterbein*
- Francis Asbury tried unsuccessfully to convert me to Methodism. *Dreisbach*

A UNITED METHODIST IS . . .

Answers

Reproducible 4B, p. 36
The History of United Methodism
1. *Wesley*; 2. *Otterbein, Boehm, Albright*; 3. *Asbury, Coke* 4. *lay representation* 5. *slavery and form of church government* 6. *The Methodist Protestant Church, The Methodist Episcopal Church, South*; 7. *Evangelical Association, United Brethren*; 8. *The United Methodist Church*

Reproducible 5A, p. 43
Three Kinds of Grace

Prevenient Grace

Read Psalm 139:13-14. When does God's love for you begin? *from the moment you are conceived*

Read Psalm 145:9. To whom is God good and for whom does God have compassion? *all*

Read Romans 5:8. According to this verse, is God's gift of grace dependent on our actions? *no*

Justifying Grace

Read Ephesians 2:8. Are we saved by our efforts to be good? *no* What is our part in salvation? *faith*

Read Romans 1:16. The word *gospel* means good news and refers to the good news of Jesus' death and resurrection for our salvation. Who can receive this gift of salvation? *all who have faith*

Read Romans 3:23-25. Justification, or saving grace, is a gift of God through whom? *Christ Jesus*

Sanctifying Grace

Read I John 3: 17-18. If God lives in us, how will that love be made known? *in truth and action*

Read 2 Corinthians 5:17. Becoming more like Christ is possible, by God's grace, because through Christ everything has <u>*become*</u> <u>*new*</u>.

Read 2 Corinthians 3:18. Having been made right with God, we are transformed into God's image. Who or what makes this transformation possible? *The Spirit of the Lord*

Reproducible 5B, p. 44
Two Sacraments

Baptism: *John (the Baptist), dove, baptizing, Father, Son, Holy Spirit*

Holy Communion: *loaf, bread, thanks, broke, body, remembrance, cup, wine, covenant, blood*

Reproducible 6B, p. 52
The United Methodist Church
- Who is the leader of an Annual Conference? *the bishop*
- How often does General Conference meet? *every four years*
- Which conference elects bishops? *the Jurisdictional Conference*
- Who assigns pastors to local churches? *the bishop, assisted by district superintendents*

Reproducible 6D, p. 60
The Least and the Lost
Matthew 9:9-13—*Matthew, the tax collector; did not approve of eating with him; Jesus ate with him*

Luke 7:36-50—*sinful woman; thought Jesus should not let a sinner touch him; forgave her sins and held her up as the good example for the way she welcomed him*

Luke 19:1-10—*Zacchaeus; criticized Jesus for going to his house; Jesus called to him, stayed with him, forgave him*

John 8:2-11—*the adulterous woman; condemned her; forgave her*

ADDITIONAL RESOURCES TO EXPAND YOUR SESSIONS

If you want to take your tweens deeper into the topics of baptism, communion, the Lord's Prayer, the Apostles' Creed, or what it means to be a Christian, you can use your choice of any or all of the What Is . . . ? books.

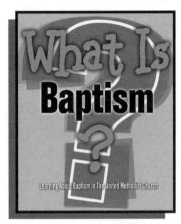

What Is Baptism?
Paperback, $2.00
ISBN: 978-0-687-49327-2

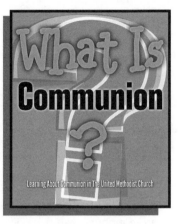

What Is Communion?
Paperback, $2.00
ISBN: 978-0-687-49337-1

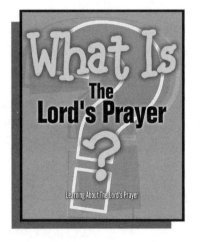

What Is the Lord's Prayer?
Paperback, $2.00
ISBN: 978-0-687-49347-0

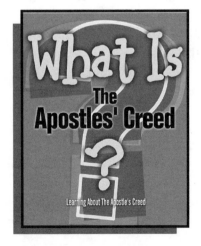

What Is the Apostles' Creed?
Paperback, $2.00
ISBN: 978-0-687-49317-3

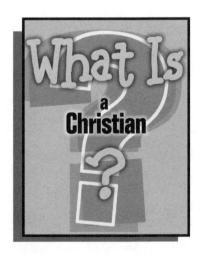

What Is a Christian?
Paperback, $2.00
ISBN: 978-0-687-49258-9

Resources can be ordered by visiting cokesbury.com; calling toll free, 800-672-1789; or writing Cokesbury Service Center, 201 Eighth Avenue, South, P.O. Box 801, Nashville, TN 37202-0801. Prices are subject to change. Use the order number given above.